Start to Draw

Animals

Written by Susannah Bradley
Illustrated by Lynne Byrnes

HENDERSON
PUBLISHING PLC
©1994 HENDERSON PUBLISHING PLC

Family Pets

Things You'll Need

pencils • drawing paper • crayons • a soft eraser

You don't need much at the beginning. Later on you can try drawing on coloured paper with chalks, including white. You can also try drawing with paint and a paintbrush.

Here are all the little ones first!

Let's start with a fish:
Copy the blue shapes first,
the body is an oval
with fins and a tail.

Use the oval shapes as guides while you draw the outline in pencil. Draw in the real details using pens or crayons.

Look at the pattern
the scales make!
Each one is the same
as the one next to it.
Fins look striped, and
they have a frilly edge.

Last of all add the eye
and a few wavy lines
for the water.

If you keep **mice** you will know that they are hardly ever still, so draw them while they are eating – it's easier!

Use ovals for the basic shape and remember to point the nose. The legs are very thin. The eyes are round and bright.

You can draw a group of mice by drawing the same mouse in different positions.

A **guinea pig's** shape is rather like a long balloon which hasn't been blown up properly. Be sure to draw his sleek fur and tiny feet with their sharp claws. His round, black eye has a white section around it and a thin black line around that.

Add some grass for a background.

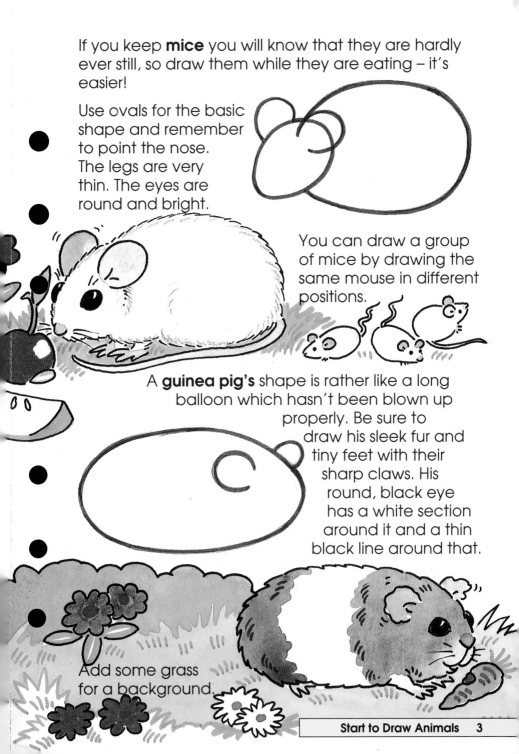

Dogs

Dogs come in so many shapes and sizes.

The best thing to do is wait until your dog is asleep, and then try drawing him.

Dogs often curl up when they are asleep. Draw the big curve his body makes. Mark lightly with your pencil the position of his head. You can use circles and ovals drawn lightly, in pencil, to start. His body will be one big oval and his head will be a small oval, on top of that.

Then draw his closed eye, his nose, and some of his fur.

Is your dog a shaggy dog? It may be long and silky, or short and wiry. Other dogs have smooth or curly coats.

How Dogs Move

Little dogs scuttle along, with their legs moving so fast that they don't seem to change position.

Big dogs take long strides, and if they have long coats their hair waves in the wind.

Some ears stand up...

...others lie flat against the head

Some have long noses...

...and some have squashed noses
Tails can be different, too.

Cats

Cats don't bounce about as much as dogs, so it is much easier to draw them!

Ovals and circles are needed again, for a sitting cat...

Tabby cats have stripes...

...a standing cat

...So do ginger ones.

A sleeping cat

Black and white cats are all marked differently.

Here is a picture of an angry cat. See how its fur stands up on its back, and how fat its tail looks!

Some cats have smooth coats but the fur on some oriental cats is long.

Cats have faces like this.

A Cat Mask

1 Make a large cardboard copy of our cat mask so that it is as wide as your face.

2 Cut it out, and cut out the eye holes, too.

3 Paint it black or white and decorate it with sequins.

4 Fix some elastic through the sides so that it fits round your head.

In the Garden

You can stay indoors, on a cold day, and draw the **birds** which come to your garden.

Yes, birds are mostly oval shapes, too! With a little practice you will find out how best to add a head to one end and a tail to the other, and you will see how birds hold their wings and feet while standing.

Here is how birds use their wings when flying.

Butterflies and Caterpillars

Butterflies come in many lovely colours, and you can use the colours and patterns of one which you have seen, or make up your own.

Here is the body. On the head, it has two feelers.

Now draw the wings on one side. There are two on each side. They can look like this...

...or this...

Trace the wings you have drawn and reverse the tracing so that you can draw the same wings on the other side of the butterfly's body.

Caterpillars are fun to draw! Look closely at one and you will see that it is made up of lots of little segments. You can draw a caterpillar which is hairy...

Munchkin

...or one which has lifted its head up and is looking around.

Pond Creatures

Snails' shells are almost round. They are spirals, really. Try drawing one like this:

Now add its head and feelers.

Dragonflies' bodies are like striped matchsticks. They have two long wings on each side of their bodies, near their heads...

...and six tiny legs.

Spiders are found all over the place. They have round bodies and heads, and eight legs.

Try drawing a hairy one with big eyes!

Frogs are fat creatures with long, thin legs. Here is one jumping...

...and here is one sitting still. See how well it folds up its legs!

Pond Pictures
Draw lots of pictures on the same page. Then you will have a busy picture with lots of things happening in it. It doesn't matter if some of the pictures don't turn out as well as you would have liked them to.

At the Farm

Use that oval shape again, whether **ducks** are bobbing about on the water, or walking around on dry land.

Draw a duck like this:

Or this:

They have big webbed feet, which help them swim.

Duck Brooches

Draw a duck on some cardboard.
Colour it, then cut it out.
Fix a small safety pin on the back with some sticky tape. Pin it on your clothes.

Geese have big, strong bodies and sturdy legs. They have long necks, and sometimes they stick them out in front to frighten other creatures away.

What makes a **chicken** look different from other birds are the fleshy lobes on top of its head and under its beak.

Cockerels are the male birds and have grander colours.

A **cow** will stand still for a long time, which makes her a good subject to draw. What is special about a cow? Udders, because cows give milk through them, of course.

Here's a cow. See what a bulky body it has, even though it has thin legs..

Another thing you might notice about a cow is its big, dark eyes.

Sheep are like woolly rectangles with heads and legs! Some have black faces.

Horses are more elegant than cows. They have strong, lean bodies and legs, and long necks. Build up the basic shape with ovals.

Then draw a jumping horse...

Back to smaller things!

A **rabbit** running for cover is too quick for an artist. You would never manage to draw it as it ran – so here is one running across the page for you to copy.

See how long its back legs are! They need to be, to push it forward.

What's special about a **squirrel**?

Its tail. The squirrel's tail curves up behind it, and is as big as the squirrel itself.

Squirrels have rounded bodies and long, sharp claws on the ends of their short legs.

A **fox** has a body like a thin dog, but its ears are large and pointed, and it has a bushy tail which is called a 'brush'.

It has a white front and belly,and the tip of its tail is white, too.

Its legs are black. A fox has a long, pointed nose and eyes which are always alert.

Because **badgers** are shy creatures you would be very lucky to see one in real life. But there's no reason why you shouldn't draw one!

The eyes and ears are in the black stripes. The rest of the body is grey.

On the Beach

Sea lions can dive more than 600ft (180m) to find food. With a soft pencil, draw the basic shapes in. What an odd looking creature!

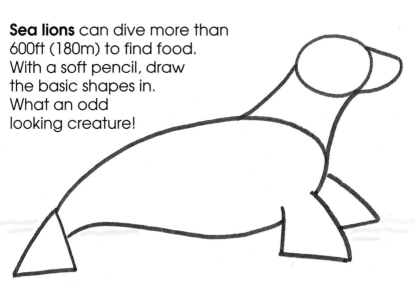

His front flipper is easy to draw if you sketch it inside a rectangle.

His back flippers use our basic triangle shape, like this:

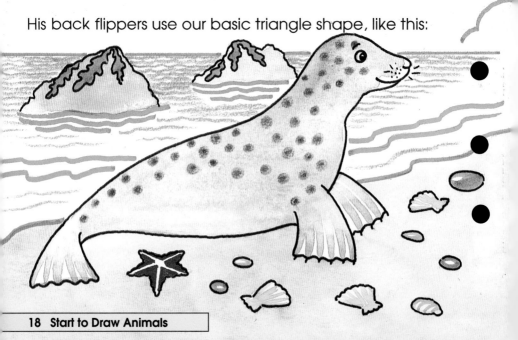

Gulls' bodies are based on ovals, like other birds, and their wings are boomerang-shaped when spread. Sometimes they bob about on the sea. They have interesting markings, like black heads, or grey tipped wings, yellow beaks and pink legs.

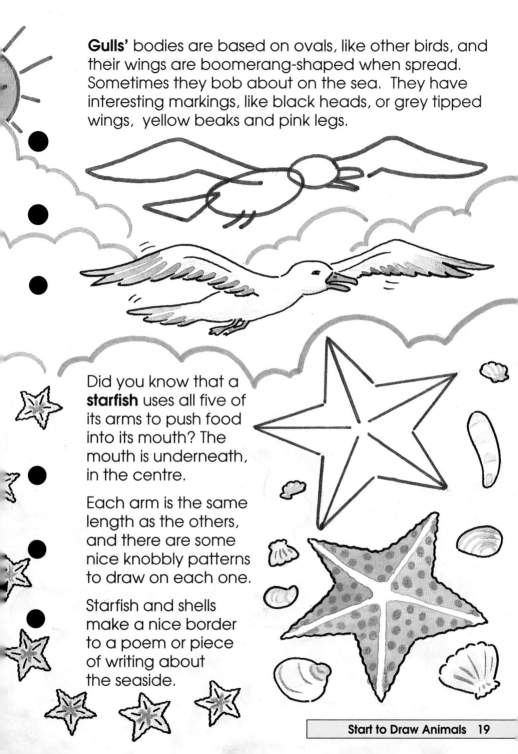

Did you know that a **starfish** uses all five of its arms to push food into its mouth? The mouth is underneath, in the centre.

Each arm is the same length as the others, and there are some nice knobbly patterns to draw on each one.

Starfish and shells make a nice border to a poem or piece of writing about the seaside.

Dinosaurs

Even though dinosaurs are no longer around, they *were* animals, and you may still want to draw one!

Here is a **stegosaurus** seen from the side. See how it is based on a curve for its back.

Dinosaurs' heads are small compared to the size of their bodies.

If you want to draw one coming towards you, it will look something like this:

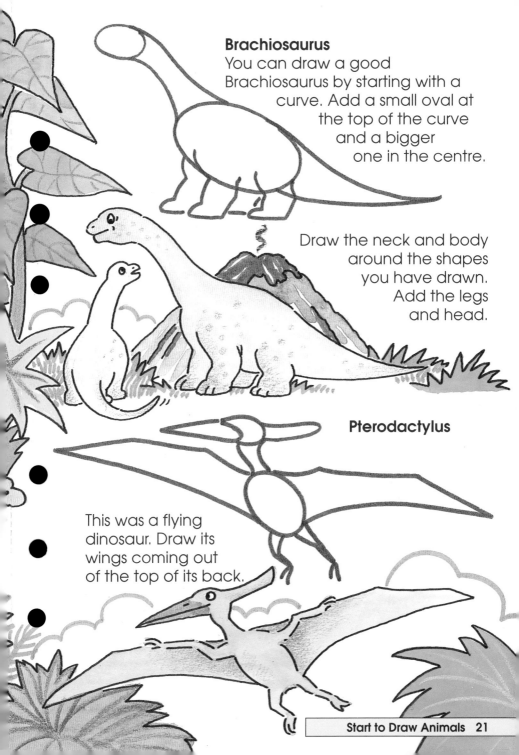

Brachiosaurus

You can draw a good
Brachiosaurus by starting with a
curve. Add a small oval at
the top of the curve
and a bigger
one in the centre.

Draw the neck and body
around the shapes
you have drawn.
Add the legs
and head.

Pterodactylus

This was a flying
dinosaur. Draw its
wings coming out
of the top of its back.

At the Zoo

In the wild, **elephants** aren't a bit cuddly. But when you draw one, it can look much more friendly!

Start with a rectangle, as we have done.

See how the trunk is wider at the top than it is at the end.

The eyes are tiny and the legs are short and fat.

Giraffes are very difficult to draw properly. The best way is to decide where you want the head to fit on the paper, and where the feet are to go.

Then fit the body and neck in between, using the shapes shown here.

A giraffe's body slopes towards its tail. It would be no use trying to ride one, even if it would let you; you would just slide off the back!

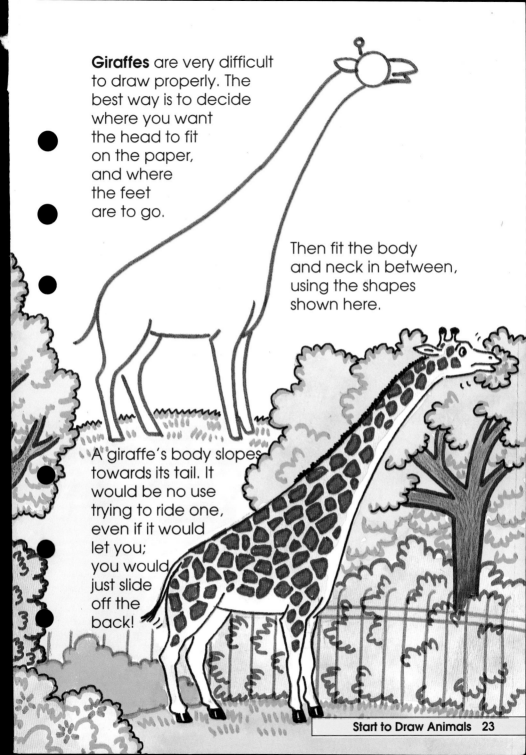

A **lion** has such a big head that
it is hard to notice anything
else about it. He has a
strong body but it is
the magnificent
mane that you
look at most.

Use shading on the body
to show how solid and
powerful these
creatures are.

Now you could try
drawing some lion cubs.

Here are two very different sea creatures!

The **dolphin** is smooth and sleek.
Its fins all curve backwards to
help it move easily through
the water. Draw an oval
first, and then add
the nose...

...the top fin...

...and the ones
which look like
tiny arms.

The **walrus** is heavy and looks awkward when seen
on land. You can have fun drawing its whiskery face
and long tusks.

It has strange
flippers instead
of feet, which it
uses to flop
across the land.

Monkeys, chimpanzees and gorillas are all different kinds of **apes**. They look a little bit like us, really! Here is a chimp for you to draw.

Here is how to draw a **chimp's** face:

First draw a pear shape:

Add two small circles above it for the eyes.

Put a nose in the top of the pear and some bags around the eyes. Add a mouth.

Draw a line round his face like this:

Now draw the dark hair all around his face, and add some ears.

The body is an oval, and the arms and legs are kidney-shaped, like this:

Use a black crayon to draw the fur. If you make the edges jagged, it will look more realistic.

Carefully draw the hands and toes. Only the fingers and toes show pink – the rest is covered with hair!

A Dancing Chimp

Make a chimp head and body out of card. Make separate arms and legs.

Make holes at the sides of his body, top and bottom, and fix the arms and legs through them, using brass paper fasteners.

Hang the chimp on your wall with a string through the top of his head. Jiggle him to make him dance.

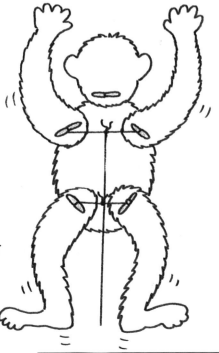

Everyone likes **penguins** and they are not difficult to draw. You start with a shape like a sack of potatoes...

...and add a head to it.

Then you draw a beak and an eye.

Add some wings at the sides.

Add the feet and claws. That's all!

Here are some penguins in other positions:

Really, you need plenty of bright felt tip pens to make a fine **parrot**. Here is the basic shape:

A Talking Parrot
Use lots of different colours to write the words round the shape of this picture. Think of things that parrots say. We have made our parrot out of some of them, but you can make your parrot say whatever you like.

The words forming the parrot shape:
SQUARK SQUARK SQUARK EEK OI PRETTY POLLY TUT TUT HELLO HELLO BYE BYE HA HA! PUT THE CAT OUT! HAVE A NICE DAY! HA HA! WHERE'S MY TEA? GOODNIGHT! I LOVE YOU TICK TOCK DING DONG COR! WHO'S A PRETTY BOY THEN! SHUT THE DOOR MERRY CHRISTMAS WOOF WOOF PIECES OF EIGHT!

A Noah's Ark

If you have tried to draw all the creatures in this book you will have lots of pictures by now. Here is a way to make them all part of one big drawing.

Use a strip of plain paper, such as the inside of a length of wallpaper. Paste two pictures of each creature to it.

Draw some scenery around them. Remember that the sea creatures will need water and the woodland ones should have trees.

Here is a picture of a Noah's ark for you to copy.

Carry on Drawing

There are lots of animals which we did not have room for in this book. What about turtles, bears and hippopotamuses? We would like to say sorry to them, and also to ostriches, armadillos and kangaroos, reindeer and rhinoceroses.

Draw whenever you can. Even take a sketchbook to the zoo – we did, while we were writing this book!

And look at other people's pictures. Copy animal pictures which you see in books. If you get lots of practice, your drawings will get better and better.

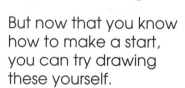

Save pictures
Cut pictures of what you like to draw out of magazines. Then you can copy the pictures. This will help you to draw better.

But now that you know how to make a start, you can try drawing these yourself.